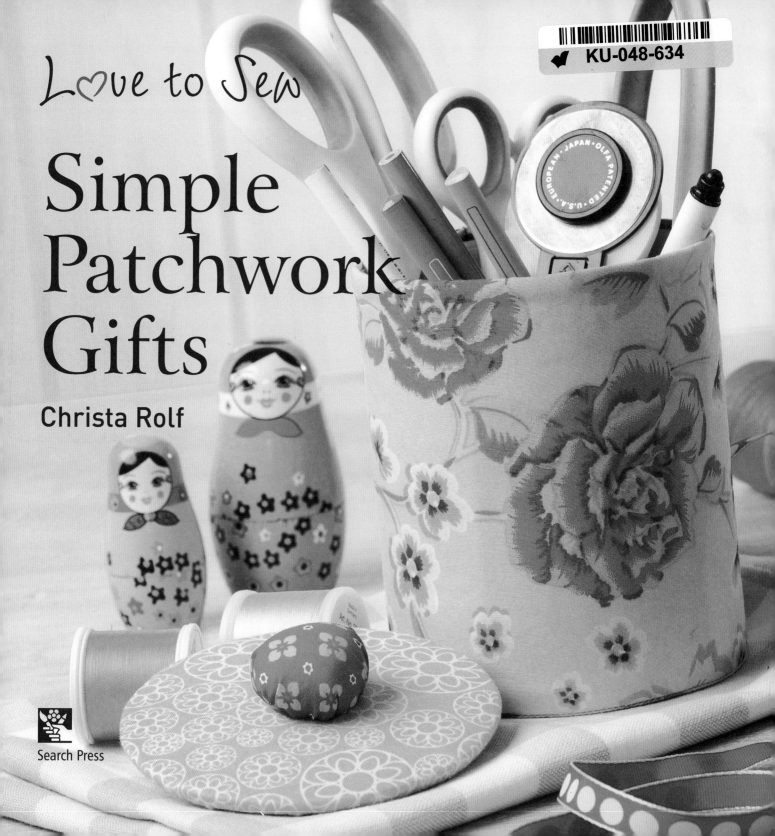

Love to Sew

Simple Patchwork Gifts

Christa Rolf

Search Press

First published in Great Britain 2014 by Search Press Limited
Wellwood, North Farm Road, Tunbridge Wells, Kent TN2 3DR

Reprinted 2014, 2015

Original German edition published as *Patch Happy!*

Copyright © 2012 Christophorus Verlag GmbH, Freiburg/Germany

Text copyright © Christa Rolf 2012

English translation by Burravoe Translation Services

ISBN: 978-1-78221-060-3

Designs: Christa Rolf
Photography: Uli Glasemann
Sewing photos: Christa Rolf
Patterns: Arnhilt Tittes
Watercolour drawings: Julia Gandras
Styling: Elke Reith

The publishers and author can accept no responsibility for any consequences arising from the information, advice or instructions given in this publication.

Acknowledgements

I would like to thank my son Niklas Rolf. With his creative intuition he was a constructive critic in the choice of colours and the design of the projects. He went without many hot meals when I sometimes wanted to sit at my sewing machine rather than standing at the cooker in the kitchen.

My thanks go to Margret Webers for her hard work and technical support on many projects.

I would also like to thank Peter Linsel, who helped me with the wording of the introduction. I always prefer playing with fabrics rather then words.

Printed in China

Table-Runner, page 14

Tea Cup Mug Rug, page 16

Pretty Butterflies, page 22

Pretty Felt Tins, page 24

Bolster Pillow, page 30

Frilly Pillow, page 32

Denim-Skirt Bag, page 44

Diary Cover, page 46

Contents

Egg Cosies, page 18

Cake Mug Rug, page 20

Teapot Mat, page 26

Lovely Pillow, page 28

Owl Pincushion, page 34

Sewing Box, page 36

Tape Measure Cover, page 40

Fabric Caddy, page 42

Laptop Bag, page 48

Phone Charm, page 52

Pencil Case, page 54

Make-up Bag, page 56

Introduction

There's no denying that patchwork sewing can bring a bit of fun and colour to everyday life. My aim is to show just how easy it is to create bright beautiful accessories for the home through the designs in this book.

I believe that all the projects reflect a cheerful, easy-going attitude to life and that the colours and patterns will brighten any home. It has been my pleasure assembing this collection, which I hope will reflect my own enjoyment of patchworking.

Most of the designs are simple to make and suitable for beginners, while the step-by-step photographs in the Sewing techniques section will help you with any slightly more difficult techniques.

Remember to have fun, enjoy the colourful patterns and the pleasure of expressing your creativity through sewing.

I wish you lots of fun and success and I hope that these projects will bring a smile to your face. They make fantastic gifts, too, and remember, a smile is the only thing that gets bigger when you give it away to someone else!

With best wishes,

Christa Roy

The projects are graded according to how easy they are:

Quick and easy ♡

Requires a little practice ♡ ♡

More challenging ♡ ♡ ♡

Materials

Fabrics

Cotton fabrics are the easiest to work with. Cotton can shrink when first washed, so the fabric should be ironed with a steam-iron before starting work. Strong colours may run when washed for the first time and should therefore be pre-washed.

Wool felt

Wool felt has its own special charm and can be used for both patchwork and appliqué. Wool felt gives motifs a three-dimensional look and the material's slightly fleecy surface makes the motifs appear soft and delicate. Unlike craft felt, wool felt may be washed with care.

Wadding/batting

Wadding/batting is used in a layer between the front and back of a project and gives designs a three-dimensional appearance. A firm, heat-stable wadding/batting is ideal for mats and pot-holders.

Fusible webbing is used to attach appliqué motifs permanently.

Adhesive fleece wadding/batting comes in various types depending on the purpose for which it is to be used.

Stabiliser is used to ensure that a fabric moves smoothly when you are machine sewing appliqué motifs. Stabiliser that can be temporarily ironed on only has a weak adhesion and can easily be removed later, which is a great help when working with felt.

Help with cutting out

The round blade of a rotary cutter cuts easily through several layers of fabric and is very useful for cutting patchwork pieces. The medium size (4.5cm/1¾in) is best for beginners.

A cutting ruler made of transparent acrylic allows you to cut accurately.

A cutting mat should be used with a rotary cutter to protect the delicate blade.

Marker pens

Water-soluble marker pens, which can be erased with a damp cloth or sponge, are useful for transferring motifs and sewing patterns.

The marker lines must be removed before ironing, otherwise unwanted traces will remain on the fabric.

Basic equipment

The following basic equipment is not specified for the individual projects, but should be available for all the projects in this book:

- ♥ Sewing machine
- ♥ Iron
- ♥ Suitable sewing thread
- ♥ Sewing needles
- ♥ Pins
- ♥ Fabric scissors
- ♥ Pencil
- ♥ Ruler

Sewing techniques

Templates

Templates are required for cutting pieces of irregular shapes that cannot be cut using a ruler and a rotary cutter. To make a template, trace or copy the pattern on to paper, paste it on to thin card and cut carefully around the outline. Place the template on the wrong side of the fabric and draw the outline (the sewing line) on to the fabric with a soft pencil. An additional seam allowance, usually 0.75cm (¼in) is required for sewing the pieces together. On curves or smaller templates it is better to use a seam allowance of only 0.5cm (⅛in). You can either add the seam allowance as you cut or draw it in by hand parallel to the outline before cutting out.

On curved templates or shapes that are difficult to match, it is helpful to have additional markings on the seam allowances. These make it easier to match up the individual pieces accurately. Cut small notches in the seam allowance or draw the marks in pencil.

Piping with and without cord

Piping may be a double strip of fabric sewn into a seam for decoration or may have a cord enclosed in the fold of the fabric. To make piping with a cord, you need fabric strips cut on the bias, which fit the cord well because they are stretchy. You can either cut the bias strips yourself from your chosen fabric or use ready-made bias binding. For the latter, iron the folds flat and trim to the desired width.

The seam allowance for sewing in piping is 1cm (½in). A cotton cord about 3mm (⅛in) diameter requires a bias strip 3cm (1¼in) wide. For thicker cords, cut the strip correspondingly wider.

When sewing in piping it is best to use the zipper foot on your machine, so you can sew as close as possible to the cord. Piping without cord can be sewn in using the normal foot.

1 Fold the strip wrong sides together and insert the cord. Pin in place and sew close to the cord.

2 To fasten the strip to an open fabric edge, simply pin in place then sew. If the piping is to go around a curve, clip the strip close to the cord at approximately 1cm (½in) intervals. This makes it easier to fit the piping around the curve.

Place the second layer of fabric on top, right sides together, and pin. Sew through all layers as close as possible to the cord.

Bindings

Binding is a way of neatening the outer edges of your work. A binding the width of a sewing machine foot of 0.75cm (¼in) is made using strips 6.5cm (2⅝in) wide.

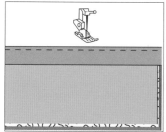 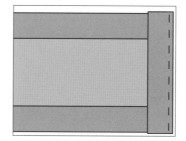

1 Cut four strips of the desired width, two of which should be the same length as the longer sides of the work. Fold the strips in half lengthways with the right sides out. With the open edges facing out, position the strips along the edges of two opposite sides, pin in place and sew the width of the foot from the edge.

2 Fold the two strips far enough over to cover the stitching in the reverse direction. Pin in place. Cut the two strips for the short sides approximately 3cm (1¼in) longer than the length of the sides. Fold in half and pin close to the remaining two opposite edges. Fold the extra 1.5cm (⅝in) at each end of the strip to the back of the fabric, around the corner. Sew the width of the foot from the edge.

3 Trim away a little of the seam allowance at the corners to prevent them from sticking out. Fold the strips far enough over to cover the stitching in the reverse direction.

4 Pin in place and stitch all four strips by hand in the shadow of the machine stitching.

Zips

A seam allowance of 1cm (½in) is needed when you are inserting a zip. Most sewing machines have a special zipper foot, which makes sewing in a zip easier. Consult the user's manual to find out which is the correct foot for your machine and what the needle position should be.

Usually the zip is sewn in with matching thread. Contrasting thread has been used for these photographs to make the seam more clearly visible.

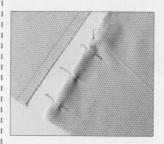 

1 Neaten the edges of the pieces of fabric for the zip. On each piece, draw a line with a water-soluble marker 1cm (½in) from the edge and parallel to it. Fold over the seam allowance for the zip along this line and tack in place.

2 Tack the zip under the fabric so that the teeth are close to the edge of the work and sew it in place using the zipper foot. Remove the tacking threads after sewing.

Bias strips and bias binding

Bias strips run diagonally to the straight grain of the fabric. This makes the strips of fabric very stretchy and particularly good for binding edges and curves. Ready-made bias binding is now available in many colours and patterns. This binding has the folds already pressed in, which makes it easier to use for binding edges.

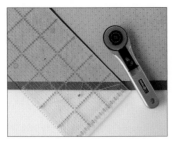

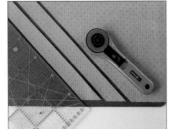

1 Spread the fabric out smoothly on a cutting mat. Place the cutting ruler at 45° to the selvedge and cut the fabric with a rotary cutter. Most cutting rulers show divisions in degrees.

2 Cut further strips of the required width parallel to this cut edge.

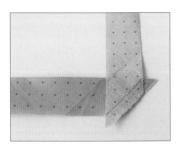

3 If you need a longer bias strip than you can cut from your length of fabric, cut several strips of the same width. To retain the elasticity, the strips should be joined at an angle of 45°(see top right). If necessary, draw a line 0.75cm (¼in) from the selvedge to help you sew.

4 Iron open the seam allowance and trim.

Making sewn-on frills

Frills will give your home-made projects a romantic look. The term describes strips of fabric that have been gathered and are sewn on to the fabric for decoration. For this type of frill, cut the fabric on the bias to prevent fraying. Frills of double fabric that are sewn into a seam can be cut on the straight grain or the bias according to your preference.

This special kind of frilling is first gathered using a gathering sewing machine foot and then sewn on to the fabric.

1 Cut bias strips approx. 1.5–2cm (½–¾in) wide and even off the ends.

Attach the gathering foot to your sewing machine and sew along the centre of the strip, which will thus be gathered. The greater the stitch length set, the more firmly the fabric will be gathered.

When you come to the end of a strip, lay the next one on top, overlapping it by about 1cm (½in). In this way you can create an infinite length of frill.

2 Change the sewing machine foot. Position the strip where you want it on the fabric and sew it in place, stitching as closely as possible to the first line of stitching.

Making sewn-in frills

These frills are often used on the outer edges of pillows. They are sewn into the seam and look particularly chunky because of the double layer of fabric. To make a frill to go round a pillow, measure the circumference of the pillow and multiply this by two.

1 Cut the strip to the desired width and sew it into a tube. Fold in half with the wrong sides together and gather along the open edges.

2 To gather, loosen the tension of the upper thread, which makes it easier to pull the lower thread later. Set the stitch length as long as possible (about 5) and sew two rows of gathering parallel and close to the outer edge. It is a good idea to use a very strong thread for the lower thread.

3 Gather the frill to the required length by pulling the two lower threads. Knot the lower threads to keep the gathers in place.

4 Pin the frill to the front of the pillow cover with the right sides together. Sew close to the edge to hold it in place. Place the pillow back on top, right sides together, sew through all the layers and turn the pillow to the right side.

Felt Appliqué

Appliqué motifs made out of felt have a three-dimensional look and their slightly fleecy surface makes them appear soft and delicate. Unlike craft felt, wool felt may be washed and it combines well with woven fabrics.

This kind of appliqué is very good for motifs that have been transferred from templates. Iron-on wadding/batting is good for templates, because the adhesive is not very strong and is easily removed.

Draw the motif on iron-on wadding/batting and fuse it to the felt. Cut through both layers exactly along the drawn outline. Pull away the wadding and attach the felt motif to the background fabric with small amounts of fabric glue. If desired, sew around the motif with running stitch or buttonhole stitch.

Table-Runner

Size: 40 x 110cm (16 x 43¼in)   Pattern layout on page 64   Difficulty level ♡♡

Materials

Cotton fabric:
- 15cm (6in) each of 18 patterned fabrics in red, white, turquoise, green, pink
- 20cm (8in) red and white striped fabric
- 45cm (18in) white backing fabric

Wadding/batting:
- 45cm (18in) thin wadding/batting

Additional items:
- 3.3m (3⅝ yards) red and white checked bias binding

Cutting out

A seam allowance of 0.75cm (¼in) is included in the cutting measurements.

From the patterned fabrics listed above, cut out:
- 37 pieces 12.5 x 12.5cm (5 x 5in)

From the red and white striped fabric, cut out:
- 2 pieces 6.5 x 112cm (2⅝ x 44in)

Tip

In patchwork shops you can often buy "charm packs" containing 12.5 x 12.5cm (5 x 5in) squares of patterned fabrics. These packs are ideal for this runner.

Method

1 Lay out the cut squares with the points upwards, alternating 1 row with 2 squares side by side and 1 row with three squares (see layout on page 64). Follow the photograph of the design or arrange your own fabrics any way you like.

2 Sew the squares together in diagonal rows and iron, with the seam allowance of each row in alternate directions.

3 Sew the rows together. Cut off the points on all the outside edges, leaving a seam allowance of 0.75cm (¼in) at the tips of the inner squares.

4 Cut 2 pieces of bias binding the length of the long sides. Iron open the folds of the bias binding, then fold each section in half lengthways and pin together. Sew together with a 0.75cm (¼in) seam allowance so they will not slip later.

5 Lay the bias binding along both long sides, right sides together. Place the strips of striped fabric right sides together on top, so that the stripe sequence is symmetrical at both ends.

6 Sew on the bias binding and edge strips in a single operation. Cut off any extra edging strip close to the edge. Iron the seam allowances of the squares so the border of checked fabric lies on top of the edging strips.

7 Cut the wadding/batting and white backing fabric a little larger than the front. Place the front and back right sides together and stitch both to the wadding/batting. Stitch together along the two long sides. Trim away the wadding/batting very close to the seam and cut the backing material to the same size as the front.

8 Turn through the runner and iron. Quilt along the squares in the shadow of the seam. On the short sides, cut the wadding/batting and backing to the size of the front and bind the open ends with the bias binding.

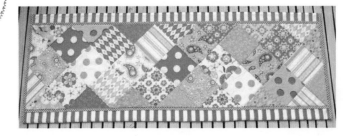

Tea Cup Mug Rug

Size: 23 x 14cm (9 x 5½in)   Pattern 1 on page 58   Difficulty level ♡♡

Materials

Cotton fabric:
- ♥ 20cm (7¾in) red patterned fabric
- ♥ 10cm (4in) turquoise patterned fabric
- ♥ Scraps of pink fabric
- ♥ 30cm (11¾in) plain fabric for backing

Wadding/batting:
- ♥ 20cm (7¾in) wadding/batting

Additional items:
- ♥ Machine quilting thread in red
- ♥ Water-soluble marker

Cutting out

The templates do not include seam allowances.

Make templates from the pattern pieces for the handle, cup and saucer. Transfer the markings for assembling it as well.

Method

1 Draw round the templates on the wrong side of the fabric and cut out, adding a 0.5cm (⅛in) seam allowance.

2 Place the pieces for the handle right sides together. Sew together along the curved edges using a short stitch length, leaving the ends that will attach to the cup open. Trim the backing fabric to the size of the front and clip the seam allowance on the curves several times close to the seam. Turn through and iron the handle.

3 Place the cup and saucer right sides together, pinning the markers on top of one another first and then the remaining fabric. Using plenty of pins will make it easier to keep the work exactly in place. Sew up the seam and fasten off the ends. Clip the seam allowance in several places and iron.

4 Pin the handle to the cup with the right sides together and sew close to the edge so that nothing can slip.

5 Place the front on a suitably sized piece of backing fabric, right sides together, with the handle between the two layers of fabric. Lay all this on a piece of wadding/batting and pin in place. Sew round the edges, leaving an opening at the top edge for turning.

6 Trim the wadding/batting close to the seam and cut the backing fabric to match the front. Clip close to the seam at the inside of the corners and around the curves. Turn the mug rug through and sew up the opening by hand.

7 Draw the curved line on the saucer freehand with the magic marker and quilt along it with the red quilting thread. Do the same in the shadow of the seam between the cup and saucer.

Tip

For curved templates it is better to add a smaller seam allowance of 0.5cm (⅛in) than a bigger one. The smaller allowance makes it easier to sew and iron the curves.

Egg Cosies

Size: approx. 9 x 9cm (3½ x 3½in)   Pattern 2 on page 58   Difficulty level ♡

Materials

Cotton fabric:
- ♥ 15cm (6in) multicoloured fabric with large spots
- ♥ 25cm (9¾in) turquoise fabric with small spots

Wadding/batting:
- ♥ 25cm (9¾in) iron-on wadding/batting

Additional items:
- ♥ 1m (39½in) red and pink checked bias binding
- ♥ 4 miniature pompoms
- ♥ Water-soluble marker

Cutting out

For 1 egg cosy
A seam allowance of 0.75cm (¼in) is included in the cutting measurements.

From the multicoloured fabric with large spots, cut out:
- ♥ 1 piece 25 x 8cm (9¾ x 3¼in)

From the turquoise fabric with small spots, cut out:
- ♥ 1 piece 25 x 4.5cm (9¾ x 2in)

Bias binding:
- ♥ Cut out 1 strip 25cm (9¾in)

Method

1 Iron the bias binding for the piping flat and cut back to a width of 2.5cm (1in). Fold in half lengthways and fasten with pins. Place the two strips of multicoloured fabric right sides together with the bias in between them and the edges matching. Sew the strips and piping together in one operation.

2 Iron over the seam allowances of the multicoloured fabric with the large spots. Cut the wadding/batting to fit the strip set you have made and iron it on to the wrong side. Top stitch along the seam between the piping and the large-spotted fabric with long stitches. Draw the pattern twice on the wadding/batting with the magic marker; the dotted line will lie on the seam between the two strips of fabric. Cut all the way around, adding a seam allowance.

3 To make the lining, draw around the pattern twice on to the turquoise fabric. When cutting out, only add seam allowance to the curves; do not add seam allowance to the bottom edge. This means the lining will be slightly smaller and will fit better inside the egg cosies.

4 Sew each egg cosy to a piece of lining along the straight edge.

5 Place the two parts right sides together and sew all the way around, leaving a small opening for turning. Clip the seam allowance on the curves close to the seam.

6 Turn through, sew up the opening and push the lining to the inside. Sew on the pompoms by hand.

Cake Mug Rug

Size: 19.5 x 16cm (7¾ x 6¼in)   Pattern 4 on page 59   **Difficulty level** ♡

Materials

Cotton fabric:
- 10cm (4in) red flowered fabric
- 10cm (4in) turquoise patterned fabric
- 25cm (9¾in) pink spotted fabric

Wadding/batting:
- 20cm (7¾in) wadding/batting

Additional items:
- 10cm (4in) wide red rickrack braid
- 1 turquoise crocheted flower

Cutting out

A seam allowance of 0.75cm (¼in) is included in the cutting measurements. The patterns do not include a seam allowance.

From the pink spotted fabric, cut out:
- 1 piece 23 x 19cm (9 x 7½in) (backing)

From the wadding/batting, cut out:
- 1 piece 23 x 19cm (9 x 7½in)

Make templates from the pattern pieces for the three tiers of the cake.

Method

1 Draw round the templates on the wrong side of the appropriate fabric, transferring the markings for assembly as well, and cut out the shapes, adding a seam allowance.

2 Sew the three tiers of the cake together, matching the markings. When sewing the individual parts together, only stitch to the corner of the seam and fasten off there. Iron, and sew on the rickrack braid roughly in the middle of the top tier.

3 Place the front and back right sides together. Lay them both on the wadding/batting and pin in place. Sew together all the way round, leaving an opening at the bottom for turning.

4 Trim the wadding/batting close to the seam and cut the backing fabric to the size of the front. Clip the insides of the corners and around the curves close to the stitching. Turn the mug rug through and sew up the opening by hand. Sew on the crocheted flower by hand.

Pretty Butterflies

Size: 6 x 6cm and 10 x 10cm (2½ x 2½ and 4 x 4in)

Pattern 3 on page 59   **Difficulty level** ♡

Materials

Cotton fabric:
- ♥ 10cm (4in) fabric with a large pattern in pink, green and white
- ♥ 10cm (4in) fabric with a large pattern in pink, green and white
- ♥ Scraps of pink and white, and green and white spotted fabric
- ♥ 20cm (7¾in) plain fabric for backing

Wadding/batting:
- ♥ Scraps of wadding/batting

Additional items:
- ♥ 10cm (4in) green cord
- ♥ Scraps of pink felt
- ♥ 1 key ring and chain
- ♥ Fabric glue
- ♥ 1 neodymium craft magnet, 1cm (½in) diameter

Cutting out

The patterns do not include a seam allowance.

Make templates from the pattern pieces for the body, wings and wing decorations (only for the fridge magnet).

Tips

If you cut the templates from transparent film it will be easier to see the grain of the fabric and to position them accurately.

Neodymium magnets are small, extra-strong magnets, that are perfect for fabric.

Method

Key ring

1 For the wings, draw once around the template on the reverse side of the pink, green and white spotted fabric and cut around it, adding a seam allowance of 0.5cm (⅛in). Place it right sides together on a second piece of fabric of the same size and lay both on a piece of wadding/batting. Sew together all the way around using a small stitch (stitch length 2).

2 Trim the wadding/batting close to the seam and cut the backing fabric to the size of the front. Clip the seam allowance on the curves close to the seam. Carefully cut a slit in the upper layer of fabric near the back end of the body area. Turn the butterfly through this opening and sew up the opening by hand.

3 Thread the key ring on to the cord and fold the cord in half. Sew it on to the top of the body area near the opening where you turned it.

4 To make the body, draw around the body template twice on the felt and cut out both pieces without adding any seam allowance. Attach to the front and back of the wings with a little fabric glue and sew all the way around, stitching through the layers with running stitch.

Fridge magnet

1 Make the wings as described for the key ring, but using the fabric with the large pattern. Insert the magnet through the opening left for turning and sew around it with small stitches through all the layers to hold the magnet firmly in place.

2 For the body and the decorations on the wings, draw the patterns on the back of the appropriate fabric and cut out, adding a seam allowance of 0.5cm (⅛in). Place each shape on a second piece of fabric, right sides together and sew the two layers together all around the edge. Make a slit in the top layer of each element and turn the shapes through. Sew up the openings by hand.

3 Position the decoration in the middle of the wing and sew it in place with small stitches. Place the body on top, with the openings to the inside, and stitch in place.

Pretty Felt Tins

Height: 4.5cm (1¾in)   **Difficulty level** ♡

Materials

Cotton fabric:
- ♥ 20cm (7¾in) fabric in red, pink or rose

Wadding/batting:
- ♥ 20cm (7¾in) iron-on wadding/batting

Additional items:
- ♥ Multicoloured cotton yarn
- ♥ Water-soluble marker
- ♥ Fabric glue
- ♥ 1cm (½in) diameter pompom each per tin in rose, pink or white
- ♥ Small tins, 4.5cm (1¾in) high and 17cm (6¾in) in circumference
- ♥ 1 sheet of pink felt for each lid

Cutting out

The measurements include a seam allowance of 0.75cm (¼in).

From the fabric, cut out:
- ♥ 1 piece 19 x 11cm (7½ x 4¼in)

From the wadding/batting, cut out:
- ♥ 1 piece 19 x 4.5cm (7½ x 1¾in)

Method

Cover for the tin

1 Iron the fabric in half, right side out. This fold line is only for use as a marker for the upper edging. Open up the fabric and iron the wadding/batting on to the reverse side of one half, positioning it a little way from the edge to leave the seam allowance free of wadding/batting.

2 Fold the fabric in half, right sides together (with the wadding/batting side to the outside) and only sew along the long edge, making a tube. Turn the tube right side out and iron. Neaten the short edges with zigzag stitch.

3 Fold the tube in half crosswise and sew the short edges together. Iron open the seam allowance. Turn through and slip it over the tin.

Lid

1 Place the lid of the tin on the felt and draw two circles around it with the magic marker. Cut out both circles, adding a 2mm (¹/₁₀in) seam allowance. Stick a piece of wadding/batting to the top of the lid with fabric glue and trim all around so that it is flush with the edge.

2 Stick one of the felt circles to the underside of the lid with a little glue and the other one on the top. Sew the two layers together all around with a row of running stitch in the multicoloured yarn. Stick a pompom on the middle of the lid with fabric glue.

Tip

Open the tins you are going to cover with a special tin opener that will not leave any sharp edges.

Teapot Mat

Size: 24 x 15cm (9½ x 6in)   **Pattern 5 on page 62**   **Difficulty level** ♡ ♡

Materials

- ♥ 20cm (7¾in) red patterned fabric
- ♥ 10cm (4in) pink checked fabric
- ♥ 10cm (4in) pink spotted fabric
- ♥ Scraps of turquoise patterned fabric
- ♥ 25cm (9¾in) plain fabric for backing

Wadding/batting:
- ♥ 20cm (7¾in) wadding/batting

Additional item:
- ♥ 1 turquoise crocheted flower
- ♥ Synthetic filling

Cutting out

The patterns do not include any seam allowance.

Make templates from the pattern pieces for the teapot, lid, handle and spout. Transfer the markings for assembling it as well.

Tip

With curved templates it is better to add a smaller seam allowance of only 0.5cm (⅛in). This makes it easier to sew and iron the curves.

Method

1 Draw round each of the templates once on the back of the appropriate fabric and cut out, adding a 0.5cm (⅛in) seam allowance.

2 Place the cut out piece for the handle right sides together on a suitably sized piece of backing fabric. Sew together along the curved edges with a small stitch length, leaving the ends that will attach to the pot open. Trim the backing fabric to the size of the front and clip the seam allowances along the curves close to the seam. Turn the handle right side out and stuff with a little filling.

3 Place the spout piece right sides together on a suitably sized piece of backing fabric and place both on a piece of wadding/batting. Sew together along the curved edges with a small stitch length, leaving the end that will attach to the pot open. Trim the wadding/batting close to the seam and the backing fabric to the size of the front. Clip the seam allowances along the curves close to the seam, turn right side out and iron.

4 Place the pieces for the pot and the lid right sides together, pinning the markers in place first and then the remainder. Using plenty of pins will make it easier to keep the work exactly in place. Sew up the seam and fasten off the ends. Clip the seam allowance in several places and iron.

5 Pin the handle and spout to the pot with the right sides together and top stitch with the narrow-edge foot so it all stays firmly in place.

6 Place the front right sides together on a suitably sized piece of backing fabric so the handle and spout will lie between the two layers of fabric. Place both layers on a piece of wadding/batting and pin together. Sew together all around, leaving an opening for turning at the bottom. Trim the wadding/batting close to the seam and cut the backing fabric to match the front. Clip close to the seam in the corners between the spout and the pot and around the curves. Turn the mat right side out and sew up the opening by hand. Top stitch in the shadow of the seam between the pot and the lid. Sew on the crocheted flower and fasten the upper part of the handle to the pot with a few hand stitches.

Lovely Pillow

Size: 50 x 30cm (19¾ x 11¾in)   Pattern 6 on pages 60-61   **Difficulty level** ♡ ♡

Materials

Cotton fabric:
- ♥ 25cm (9¾in) red fabric
- ♥ 30cm (11¾in) pink and white checked fabric
- ♥ 10cm (4in) each of 6 different patterned fabrics in red, pink and white

Additional items:
- ♥ 30 x 40cm (11¾ x 15¾in) sheet of red felt
- ♥ Scraps of rose and pink felt
- ♥ 175cm (69in) red bias binding
- ♥ Fabric glue

Cutting out

A seam allowance of 0.75cm (¼in) is included in the patterns.

From the red fabric, cut out:
- ♥ 2 pieces 52 x 23cm (20½ x 9in) for the backing fabric

From the checked patterned fabrics, cut out:
1st strip 35 x 5.5cm (13¾ x 2¼in)
2nd strip 35 x 5.5cm (13¾ x 2¼in)
3rd strip 35 x 8.5cm (13¾ x 3⅜in)
4th strip 35 x 3.5cm (13¾ x 1½in)
5th strip 35 x 11.5cm (13¾ x 4½in)
6th strip 35 x 5.5cm (13¾ x 2¼in)
7th strip 35 x 3.5cm (13¾ x 1½in)
8th strip 35 x 8.5cm (13¾ x 3⅜in)
9th strip 35 x 5.5cm (13¾ x 2¼in)
10th strip 35 x 3.5cm (13¾ x 1½in)
11th strip 35 x 5.5cm (13¾ x 2¼in)

For the strips of pink and white checked fabric, first cut across the fabric on the bias (i.e. at an angle of 45°) and then cut parallel strips of the required sizes.

Method

1 Arrange the strips as in the sketch below. Begin by sewing groups of two strips together and neatening the edges of the seam allowance with zigzag stitch.

2 Then sew pairs of these together so that four strips are joined and so on until all the strips have been joined. This method will prevent the strips from pulling out of shape. Neaten all the seam allowances with zigzag stitch. Trim down the front of the pillow cover to a height of 31.5cm (12½in).

3 Transfer the patterns for the individual letters to the red felt and cut them out with no seam allowance (see Sewing techniques, page 13). Arrange them on the pillow cover and attach them with a little fabric glue. Top stitch around all the edges with short stitches (stitch length 1.5–2). Cut the small heart out of rose felt and the bigger heart in pink felt. Glue them in the middle of the 'O' and edge stitch.

4 For the envelope closure on the back of the pillow, fold over a double hem of 1cm (½in) along one long edge of each of the red fabric backing pieces and top stitch. Place the two backing pieces together, with the hemmed edges overlapping far enough to make the back the same size as the front. Place the pillow cover on top of them, wrong sides together, and sew around the edges. Trim the back to the exact size of the front.

5 Bind all the edges with bias binding.

Bolster Pillow

Size: approx. 13 x 35cm (5 x 13¾in)   **Difficulty level** ♡ ♡

Materials

Cotton fabric
- ♥ 50cm (19¾in) fabric in turquoise with large pattern
- ♥ 15cm (6in) fabric in turquoise and white stripes
- ♥ 15cm (6in) turquoise fabric

Additional items:
- ♥ 1m (39½in) pink and white checked bias binding
- ♥ 1m (39½in) pink bias binding
- ♥ 1m (39½in) 4mm (¹/₈in) pink satin cord
- ♥ 2m (79in) cotton cord, 4mm (¹/₈in) in diameter, for piping
- ♥ 1 foam bolster pad 13 x 35cm (5 x 13¾in)

Cutting out

A seam allowance of 1cm (½in) is included in the measurements.

From the fabric in turquoise with large pattern, cut out:
- ♥ 1 piece 22 x 43cm (8¾ x 17in)

From the fabric in turquoise and white stripes, cut out:
- ♥ 2 pieces 9.5 x 43cm (3¾ x 17in)

From the fabric turquoise fabric, cut out:
- ♥ 2 pieces 9.5 x 43cm (3¾ x 17in)

From the pink and white checked bias binding, cut out:
- ♥ 2 lengths of 43cm (17in)

From the pink bias binding, cut out:
- ♥ 2 lengths of 43cm (17in)

From the cotton cord, cut out:
- ♥ 4 lengths of 43cm (17in)

Method

1 For the piping, iron open the folds of the bias binding. Trim to a width of 3cm (1¼in), fold in half and place the cotton cord inside. Pin in place and sew close to the cord (see Sewing techniques, page 10).

2 Sew the fabric pieces together to form a striped pattern, following the sketch below. Sew the two pink piping strips to the central piece and the checked piping in the other two seams. Neaten the seam edges with zigzag stitch.

3 Fold the strip set that you have created in half, right sides together, and sew up the long seam, neatening the edges. On the two outer edges, fold over a double hem of 1cm (½in) and top stitch along the edge. Leave a small opening in the outer edge of the seam for threading the cord into the channel and turn through.

4 Cut the satin cord into two even lengths and thread them through the channels with the help of a safety pin. Insert the pillow pad in the cover. Pull the satin cords tight and tie the ends in a bow.

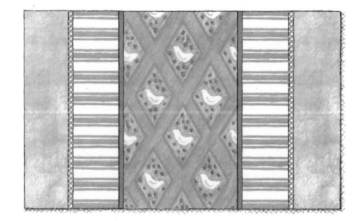

Materials

Cotton fabric:
- ♥ 65cm (25½in) fabric in red with large roses
- ♥ 10cm (4in) fabric in red with small roses
- ♥ 25cm (9¾in) pink and white patterned fabric

Additional items:
- ♥ 2.5m (2¾ yards) red and white checked bias binding
- ♥ 1m (39½in) white lace trim
- ♥ Gathering foot for the sewing machine

Cutting out

A seam allowance of 0.75cm (¼in) is included in the measurements.

From the fabric in red with large roses, cut out:
- ♥ 1 piece 22 x 22cm (8¾ x 8¾in) (front)
- ♥ 2 pieces 42 x 33cm (16½ x 13in) (back)
- ♥ 3 pieces 10 x 110cm (4 x 43¼in) (frill)

From the fabric in red with small roses, cut out:
- ♥ 2 pieces 5.5 x 22cm (2¼ x 8¾in)
- ♥ 2 pieces 5.5 x 30cm (2¼ x 11¾in)

From the pink and white patterned fabric, cut out:
- ♥ 2 pieces 22.5 x 22.5cm (9¼ x 9¼in)

Frilly Pillow

Size: 40 x 40cm (15¾ x 15¾in) (not including frill)   **Difficulty level** ♡ ♡

Method

Pillow

1 For the front, sew the strip of fabric patterned with small roses around the centre square (see sketch below, left). Neaten all the seams with zigzag stitch.

2 Cut the two squares of the pink and white patterned fabric in half diagonally to make four triangles for the corners. First sew two triangles to two opposite sides and then the remaining two to the other sides, following the sketches. Stitch the white lace, along the edges of the central square, making a mitre in the corners. Do this for both the back and the front pieces.

3 Round off the corners of the front of the pillow cover with the help of a jar approximately 8cm (3¼in) in diameter.

4 To make the envelope closure on the back of the pillow, fold over a double hem of 1cm (½in) along one long edge of each of the backing pieces and top stitch. Place the two backing pieces together, with the hemmed edges overlapping far enough to make the back the same size as the front, including the rounding of the corners, and pin in place.

Frills

1 To make the narrow frills on the front of the pillow, iron the bias binding open and cut to a width of 1.5cm (¾in). Fit the gathering foot to your sewing machine and sew along the strips to gather them (see Sewing techniques, page 12). Sew on to the seams between the triangles and the red centre. At the end of the seam, cut off the strip close to the edge of the fabric.

2 For the broad frills around the edge of the pillow, cut the three strips on the bias at 45° and sew together to make one long strip (see Sewing techniques, page 12). Cut the strip to a length of 3.2m (3½ yards) and form into a tube: fold the strip in half, wrong sides together, and gather along the open edges (see Sewing techniques, page 13).

3 Gather to fit the circumference of the pillow. Pin to the front of the pillow, right sides together. Sew close to the edge. Place the pillow back on top with the right sides together and sew.

4 Neaten the edges with zigzag stitch. Turn through the pillow cover and iron.

Owl Pincushion

Height: 13cm (5in)   Pattern 7 on page 63   **Difficulty level** ♡

Pattern 7 on page 63

Materials

Cotton fabric:
- ♥ 20cm (7¾in) turquoise and white spotted fabric
- ♥ Scraps of turquoise patterned and pink checked fabric
- ♥ 20cm (7¾in) plain fabric for backing

Wadding/batting:
- ♥ Scraps of wadding/batting

Additional items:
- ♥ Scraps of pink, white and beige felt
- ♥ Synthetic stuffing
- ♥ 10cm (4in) pink ric-rac braid
- ♥ 2 black 4mm (⅛in) beads
- ♥ 2 buttons
- ♥ Fabric glue
- ♥ Rice

Cutting out

The patterns do not include seam allowance.

Make templates from the patterns.

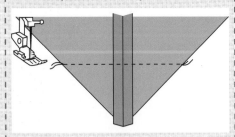

Method

1 For the appliqué pocket, draw the pattern once on the back of the turquoise patterned fabric and cut out, adding a seam allowance of 0.5cm (⅛in). Sew on the ric-rac braid 2cm (¾in) from the upper edge. Place right sides together on a suitably sized piece of backing fabric.

2 Sew together all around with small stitches (stitch length 2), leaving an opening in the upper edge for turning. Cut the backing fabric to the size of the front. Clip the seam allowance on the curves several times close to the stitching. Turn right side out and sew up the opening by hand.

3 For the body, draw the pattern once on the back of the turquoise and white fabric, transferring the markings for the bottom corners as well. Cut out, adding a seam allowance of 0.5cm (⅛in). Stitch on the pocket 4cm (1½in) from the bottom of the body, leaving the top edge free to open. Place right sides together on to the backing fabric.

4 Sew together all around with small stitches (stitch length 2), leaving an opening for turning as indicated by the dashes at the top of the template. Sew across the bottom corners (see sketch below, left). Cut the backing fabric to the size of the front.

5 Clip the seam allowance on the curves several times close to the stitching and turn. Fill with rice to start with, so the owl will stand more firmly. Then stuff firmly with the synthetic filling and sew up the opening by hand.

6 Transfer the patterns for the eye background, eyes and beak to the felt and cut out without seam allowance (see Sewing techniques, page 13). Fix in place with fabric glue and sew on the two beads by hand.

7 For the wings, draw the pattern twice on the back of the pink checked fabric and cut out, adding a seam allowance of 0.5cm (⅛in). Place each one right sides together on a suitably sized piece of backing fabric, then both together on a piece of wadding/batting. Sew together all around with small stitches (stitch length 2), leaving an opening for turning. Cut the backing fabric to the size of the front and trim the wadding/batting close to the seam. Clip the seam allowance on the curves several times close to the stitching. Turn through and sew up the opening by hand.

8 Sew the wings to the sides of the body with the buttons, using a few hand stitches to keep everything in place.

Materials

Cotton fabric:
- 💜 30cm (11¾in) turquoise fabric with roses
- 💜 30cm (11¾in) pink fabric

Wadding/batting and interfacing:
- 💜 45cm (17¾in) double-sided iron-on wadding/batting
- 💜 45cm (17¾in) lightweight iron-on interfacing

Additional items:
- 💜 125cm (49¼in) pink spotted bias binding
- 💜 125cm (49¼in) pink checked bias binding
- 💜 125cm (49¼in) cotton cord, 4mm (⅛in) diameter, for the piping
- 💜 50cm (19¾in) pink ric-rac braid
- 💜 1 turquoise zip, 45cm (18in) long
- 💜 20cm (7¾in) pink webbing
- 💜 2 pink crocheted flowers
- 💜 20cm (7¾in) pink cord
- 💜 1 small wooden cotton reel
- 💜 50cm (19¾in) pink 1cm (½in) elastic
- 💜 Water-soluble marker

Cutting out

From the turquoise fabric, cut out:
- 💜 1 piece 42 x 25cm (16½ x 9¾in) (top and bottom)
- 💜 1 piece 50 x 20cm (19¾ x 7¾in) (sides)

From the pink fabric, cut out:
- 💜 1 piece 42 x 25cm (16½ x 10in) (top and bottom)
- 💜 1 piece 50 x 20cm (19¾ x 7¾in) (sides)

From the wadding/batting, cut out:
- 💜 1 piece 42 x 25cm (16½ x 9¾in) (top and bottom)
- 💜 1 piece 50 x 20cm (19¾ x 7¾in) (sides)

From the lightweight interfacing, cut out:
- 💜 1 piece 42 x 25cm (16¼ x 9¾in) (top and bottom)
- 💜 1 piece 50 x 20cm (19¾ x 7¾in) (sides)

Sewing Box

Size: 20 x 12 x 12cm (7¾ x 4¾ x 4¾in)   Difficulty level ♡ ♡ ♡

Templates

For the top and bottom, draw a rectangle 36 x 20cm (14¼ x 7¾in) on paper and mark the centre points of each side. Round off the four corners with the aid of a jar 8cm (3¼in) in diameter. For the sides, draw a rectangle 44 x 12cm (17¼ x 4¾in), mark the centres of the sides and round off the corners. Draw a line 4cm (1½in) from the upper edge for the zip. Cut out the patterns.

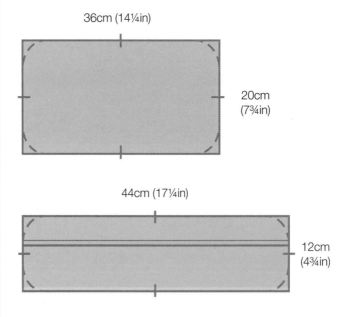

36cm (14¼in)

20cm (7¾in)

44cm (17¼in)

12cm (4¾in)

Method

1 For the top and bottom of the box, spread out the pink fabric, wrong side up. Place the interfacing (fusible side down) on top, then the wadding/batting, and lastly the turquoise fabric, right side up. Cover the layers with a damp cloth and iron them together. Repeat the process with the side piece.

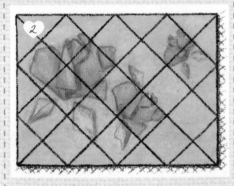

2 On the right side of the two pieces of turquoise fabric draw two intersecting lines at 45° to the edge. Stitch along both lines with a straight stitch (stitch length 3). With the aid of a quilting ruler, stitch parallel lines 4cm (1½in) apart to cover the whole surface.

3 Cut through the side piece 7cm (2¾in) from the upper edge and insert the zip (see Sewing techniques, page 11). Place the pattern pieces on the back of the fabric, transfer the markers for the zip and centre points, and cut out, adding a 1cm (½in) seam allowance. Sew on the ric-rac braid 2cm (¾in) below the zip.

4 For the piping, iron open the pink spotted bias binding and trim the whole length to a width of 3cm (1¼in). Make the piping with the cotton cord (see Sewing techniques, page 10). Sew the piping to the top and bottom of the sewing box, taking care to stitch just inside the seam allowance.

5 Open the zip, pin the side piece to the top and bottom, matching the markers, and sew together. Trim the seam allowance to 0.5cm (⅛in) and sew the pink checked bias binding over the seam allowance by hand to cover it.

Finishing

Fold in the ends of the webbing by about 2cm (¾in) and stitch to the top of the box to make a handle. Sew on the crocheted flowers. Thread the pink cord through the zip pull, thread both ends through the cotton reel and knot the ends together. Sew the elastic to the inside at the level of the rick-rack braid, to make loops to hold your own sewing gear.

Tip

If your sewing machine does not have a quilting ruler, draw the lines on the fabric with the water-soluble marker.

Tape Measure Cover

Size: 6 x 7cm (2½ x 2¾in)   Pattern 8 on page 62   Difficulty level ♡

Materials

Cotton fabric:
- ♥ 10cm (4in) multicoloured fabric
- ♥ 10cm (4in) red spotted fabric

Wadding/batting
- ♥ 10cm (4in) wadding/batting

Additional items:
- ♥ Scraps of green felt
- ♥ 30cm (11¾in) small pompom braid in pink
- ♥ 30cm (11¾in) pink cord
- ♥ 1 flower-shaped button
- ♥ 1 self-winding tape measure
- ♥ Fabric glue

Cutting out

A seam allowance of 0.75cm (¼in) is included in the measurements. The patterns do not include seam allowance.

Make templates from the patterns for the house and the house plus roof.

Note: These instructions refer to the house with the red roof pictured opposite.

Red spotted fabric:
2 pieces 4 x 9cm (1½ x 3½in)
2 pieces 4 x 11cm (1½ x 4¼in)

Tip

If you cut the templates from transparent film it will be easier to see the grain of the fabric and to position them accurately.

Method

1 Draw around the template for the house on the back of the multicoloured fabric and cut out, adding a seam allowance. Place the shorter red strips of the sloping roof on the top left and bottom right of the multicoloured patterned fabric.

2 Pin in place and sew along the markings on the pattern. Fold the strips over and iron with a dry iron. Extend the markings for the sloping roof on to the back of these strips with the aid of a ruler.

3 Sew the longer red strips along this line, right sides together, and iron open. On the wrong side of the fabric trace the template for the house plus roof and cut out, adding a seam allowance.

4 Place this, right sides together, on a suitably sized piece of the red spotted fabric and place both on a piece of wadding/batting. Sew all around with a small stitch (stitch length 2), leaving an opening for turning. Trim the wadding/batting close to the seam and cut the backing fabric to the size of the front. Trim away the seam allowance at the corners. Turn the house right side out and sew up the opening by hand.

5 Top stitch the seam between the roof and the house. Attach the pompom braid along the edge of the roof, leaving a little extra braid at each end. Fold this extra to the back and stitch on by hand.

6 Fold the house in half and sew up both side edges with invisible stitches. Insert the tape measure and sew up the edges of the sloping roof.

7 For the circle, draw around a coin on the felt and cut out without adding seam allowance. Sew the button to the felt. Glue the circle to the house at the point where the push-button is located on the tape measure, if it has one. Pull the tape a little way out of the cover. Make a hole just below the metal tab with a thick needle or cut one with a sharp pair of scissors. Thread the cord through the hole and knot the ends together. Fold up the bottom corners of the house and sew in place with a few hand stitches.

Fabric Caddy

Height: 12cm (4¾in)   Difficulty level ♡

Materials

Cotton fabric:
- 💗 30cm (11¾in) flowered turquoise fabric
- 💗 30cm (11¾in) turquoise patterned fabric
- 💗 Scraps of red patterned fabric

Wadding/batting:
- 💗 20cm (7¾in) iron-on wadding/batting

Additional items:
- 💗 Scraps of synthetic stuffing
- 💗 Fabric glue
- 💗 Strong sewing thread
- 💗 1 tin 12cm (4¾in) tall and 32cm (12½in) in circumference

Cutting out

A seam allowance of 0.75cm (¼in) is included in the measurements.

From the turquoise flowered fabric, cut out:
- 💗 1 piece 34 x 26cm (13½ x 10¼in)

From the wadding/batting, cut out:
- 💗 1 piece 34 x 12cm (13½ x 4¾in)

Tip

Open the tins you are going to cover with a special tin opener that will not leave any sharp edges.

Method

Cover for the tin

1 Fold the turquoise flowered fabric in half lengthways, wrong sides together and iron. This crease only serves as a marker for the upper edge. Open up the fabric and fuse the wadding/batting to one half, positioning the wadding/batting a little way from the crease so there is no wadding/batting on the seam allowance.

2 Fold the fabric in half, right sides together (so the wadding/batting will be on the outside), and sew along the long edge to form a tube. Turn the tube the right way out and iron. Neaten the short edges with zigzag stitch.

3 Fold the tube in half crossways and sew the short edges together. Iron open the seam allowance. Turn and slip the tube over the tin.

Fabric lid

1 For the underside of the lid, draw twice around the lid on the wrong side of the turquoise patterned fabric and cut it out without adding seam allowance. Cut a slit for turning in one of the pieces. Place this circle on the other, right sides together, and place both on a piece of wadding/batting. Sew all around through all layers. Trim the wadding/batting close to the seam and clip the fabric close to the stitching. Turn through and iron.

2 For the upper side of the lid, place the tin lid on the wrong side of the turquoise patterned fabric and draw around it with a soft pencil. Draw a 2.5cm (1in) seam allowance all around and cut out. Cut a circle of wadding/batting the same size.

3 Glue some wadding/batting to the top of the lid and cut away close to the edge.

4 Sew round the edge of the circle of wadding/batting with strong thread and a long running stitch, starting with a knot and a backstitch. When you have gone full circle, pull the thread gently to gather the wadding/batting a little. Pull the thread tight and sew in the end. Follow the same procedure with the circle of fabric, pull it over the lid and stitch to secure.

5 On the underside, sew the smaller fabric circle to the other fabric by hand, with the opening for turning on the inside.

6 For the bobble, cut a circle of red fabric 7–8cm (2¾–3¼in) in diameter. Gather around the edge, pull the thread a little and stuff with filling. Pull the thread tight and stitch it to the middle of the lid.

Materials

Cotton fabric 140cm (55in) wide:
- ♥ 40cm (15¾in) pink and white spotted fabric
- ♥ 45cm (17¾in) pink and white checked fabric
- ♥ 10cm (4in) pink and white striped fabric

Additional items:
- ♥ 1 small pair denim jeans
- ♥ 15cm (6in) pink ric-rac braid
- ♥ 20cm (7¾in) pink frilled edging
- ♥ 3.3m (3¼ yards) white lace trim 1cm (½in) wide
- ♥ 1m (39½in) white lace trim 1.5cm (¾in) wide
- ♥ 1 pink crocheted flower
- ♥ Assorted buttons
- ♥ Small lace motifs

Cutting out

A seam allowance of 0.75cm (¼in) is included in the measurements.

From the pink and white spotted fabric, cut out:
- ♥ 2 pieces 79 x 18cm (31 x 7in) for the outside

From the pink and white checked fabric, cut out:
- ♥ 2 pieces 3.5 x 75cm (1½ x 29½in) for the handles
- ♥ 2 pieces 45 x 32cm (17¾ x 12½in) for the lining

From the pink and white striped fabric, cut out:
- ♥ 1 piece 8 x 125cm (3¼ x 49¼in) for the belt

From the denim (trouser legs), cut out:
- ♥ 2 pieces 6.5 x 75cm (2½ x 29½in) for the handles

Denim-Skirt Bag

Size: 41 x 34cm (16¼ x 13½in)   Measurement diagram on page 64

Difficulty level ♡

Method

1 Cut the legs off the jeans about 2cm (¾in) below the zip. Place the front and back lower edges of the body of the jeans exactly on top of one another and even up if necessary. The circumference at the lower edge should be about 90cm (35½in). Stitch the pink frilled edging along one of the pocket openings. Stitch the strip of narrow white lace trim to the other pocket opening. Stitch on the ric-rac braid and sew on a couple of buttons by hand.

2 To make the lower part of the bag, round off the bottom corners of the two pieces of pink spotted fabric by drawing around a small plate. Place the two pieces right sides together and sew up the seams at the bottom and sides. Mark the centre of the front and back and, starting from there, mark in the fold and placement lines on the fabric as shown on the diagram on page 64.

3 Make folds at the 4cm (1½in) marks following the same diagram, position the folds on the placement lines and pin in place. Pin the lower part to the upper part of the jeans right sides together and sew the fabrics together. If necessary, adjust the width of the outer pleats and turn the bag right side out.

4 Sew on the wide lace just above the seam. Sew on the crocheted flower by hand.

5 To make each of the handles, place a strip of denim and a strip of checked fabric right sides together, matching one long edge and sew together. Adjust it so that the other long edges match and sew these together. Turn through the handle and iron so that the strip of checked fabric runs along the middle. Top stitch in the shadow of the seams. Sew on the narrow lace to the right and left of the checked fabric.

6 Repeat to make the second handle. Neaten the ends of the handles and stitch these to the inside of the jeans at the waistband.

7 For the lining, round off the bottom corners of the two remaining pieces of pink and white checked fabric in the same way as for the bottom of the bag. Place them right sides together and sew, leaving the top edge open. Fold over 1cm (½in) along the top edge to the wrong side and hand stitch to the bottom edge of the jeans' waistband, reducing any extra width by making one or two small pleats. Tuck the lining inside the bag.

8 To make the belt, fold the strip of pink and white striped fabric in half lengthways with the right sides together. Sew up, leaving a small opening for turning. Turn through and top stitch all around, close to the edges. Thread the belt through the loops and tie in a knot.

Diary Cover

Size: 11 x 15.5cm (4¼ x 6¼in), 1.5cm (½in) high   **Difficulty level** ♡ ♡

Materials

Cotton fabric:
- ♥ 10cm (4in) turquoise spotted fabric
- ♥ 20cm (7¾in) turquoise paisley fabric

Wadding/batting:
- ♥ 20cm (7¾in) iron-on wadding/batting

Additional items:
- ♥ 50cm (19¾in) red and white checked bias binding
- ♥ 50cm (19¾in) white lace trim
- ♥ 20cm (8in) white elastic, 1cm (½in) wide
- ♥ 60cm (24in) white satin ribbon, 3mm (¼in) wide
- ♥ 1 diary 11 x 15.5cm (4¼ x 6¼in), 1.5cm (½in) thick
- ♥ 1 crocheted flower
- ♥ 3 pompoms

Cutting out

A seam allowance of 0.75cm (¼in) is included in the measurements.

From the turquoise spotted fabric, cut out:
- ♥ 1 piece 46 x 6cm (18 x 2½in) for the outside

From the turquoise paisley fabric, cut out:
- ♥ 1 piece 46 x 13cm (18 x 5in) for the outside
- ♥ 1 piece 12 x 16.5cm (4¾ x 6½in) for the inside

From the wadding/batting, cut out:
- ♥ 1 piece 25 x 16.5cm (10 x 6½in)

Method

1 Iron open the bias binding for the edging, fold in half lengthways and pin. Sew together with a 5mm (¼in) seam allowance to prevent it from slipping. Place the two paisely pieces for the outside right sides together, with the bias binding between them matching the edges. Sew the strips and binding together in a single operation. Iron the seam allowance towards the turquoise spotted fabric. Sew on the lace about 1cm (½in) from the binding. Fuse the wadding/batting on to the middle of the wrong side of the fabric as shown below.

2 Neaten the short outer edges of the fabric with zigzag stitch. Fold over 1cm (½in) for the seam allowance and top stitch close to the edge.

3 With pins, mark off 24cm (9½in) for the total width of the diary. Pin on the elastic 3cm (1¼in) from the back edge. Divide the satin ribbon into three strips of 20cm (7¾in) and pin them in the middle.

4 Fold the fabric to the front at the markers. These parts of the fabric will later form the openings for the cover.

5 Neaten the 16.5cm (6½in) edges of the inside piece with zigzag stitch. Fold in the two outside flaps so the wrong sides are facing you, with the right side of the fabric showing in the centre. Stitch together along the upper and lower edges.

 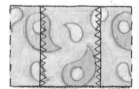

6 Cut away the seam allowance at the corners. Turn the cover right side out and slide the diary into it. Put the satin ribbon into the diary and cut to different lengths. Glue a pompom to the end of each ribbon. Fold the elastic to the front and sew on the crocheted flower.

Laptop Bag

Size: 42 x 30cm (16½ x 11¾in)   Pattern 9 on page 63   Difficulty level ♡ ♡ ♡

Materials

Cotton fabric:
- ♥ 40cm (15¾in) denim fabric
- ♥ 50cm (19¾in) red fabric with roses
- ♥ 20cm (7¾in) fabric with large roses

Wadding/batting and interfacing:
- ♥ 70cm (27½in) double-sided iron-on wadding/batting
- ♥ 40cm (15¾in) lightweight iron-on interfacing

Additional items:
- ♥ 75cm (29½in) lining fabric
- ♥ 3m (3⅜ yards) pink bias binding
- ♥ 3m (3⅜ yards) cotton cord, 4mm (¹/₈in) diameter, for piping
- ♥ 50cm (19¾in) pink ric-rac braid
- ♥ 20cm (7¾in) pink satin ribbon, 1cm (½in) wide
- ♥ 15cm (6in) pink satin ribbon, 4mm (¹/₈in) wide
- ♥ 1 pink zip, length 60cm (23½in)
- ♥ 1 pair 70cm (27½in) handles
- ♥ 1 wooden bead
- ♥ Assorted buttons and lace motifs
- ♥ 1 water-soluble marker
- ♥ Fabric glue

Cutting out

A seam allowance of 1cm (½in) is included in the measurements.

From the denim, cut out:
- ♥ 2 pieces 44.5 x 35cm (17½ x 13¾in) for the front and back

From the red fabric with roses, cut out:
- ♥ 2 pieces 20 x 30cm (7¾ x 11¾in) for the pocket and back
- ♥ 1 piece 82 x 12cm (32¼ x 4¾in) for the bottom and sides
- ♥ 1 piece 67 x 14cm (26½ x 5½in) for the zip opening

From the fabric with large roses, cut out:
- ♥ 1 piece 20 x 30cm (7¾ x 11¾in) for a machine appliqué of your choice

From the lining fabric, cut out:
- ♥ 2 pieces 44.5 x 35cm (17½ x 13¾in) for the front and back
- ♥ 1 piece 82 x 12cm (32½ x 4¾in) for the bottom and sides
- ♥ 1 piece 67 x 14cm (26½ x 5½in) for the zip opening

From the lining fabric wadding/batting, cut out:
- ♥ 2 pieces 44.5 x 35cm (17¼ x 13¾in) for the front and back
- ♥ 1 piece 82 x 12cm (32¼ x 4¾in) for the bottom and sides
- ♥ 1 piece 67 x 14cm (26½ x 5½in) for the zip opening
- ♥ 1 piece 20 x 30cm (7¾ x 11¾in) for a machine appliqué of your choice

From the lightweight interfacing, cut out:
- ♥ 2 pieces 44.5 x 35cm (17¼ x 13¾in) for the front and back

Pattern

For the front and back, draw a rectangle 42 x 30cm (16½ x 11¾in) on a sheet of paper, marking the mid-points of the outer edges (see below). Round off the corners with the aid of the pattern on page 63.

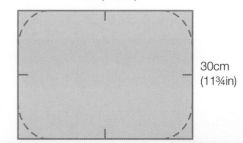

42cm (16½in)

30cm (11¾in)

Method

1 For the front and back, spread out the denim fabric, wrong side up. Place the interfacing (fusible side down) on top of it, then the wadding/batting and lastly the lining fabric, right side up. Cover the layers with a damp cloth and iron together. Repeat the same procedure for the bottom and side pieces, but without interfacing.

2 With the water-soluble marker, draw two intersecting lines at 45° to the edge on the right side of the two pieces of denim. Stitch along both lines with a straight stitch (stitch length 3). With the aid of a quilting ruler, stitch parallel lines 4cm (1½in) apart to cover the whole surface, following the sketch on page 38. Repeat the process with the fabric pieces for the bottom and sides of the bag and the zip opening.

3 Draw the pattern on the wrong side of the front and back pieces, transferring the markings for the mid-points, and cut out, adding a 1cm (½in) seam allowance.

4 Sew the ric-rac braid to the front of the bag, about 9cm (3½in) from the upper edge. For the machine appliqué, fuse the wadding/batting to the back of the fabric with the large roses, covering the other fusible side with greaseproof paper. Cut out the rose motif, position it and iron in place. Attach smaller flower motifs to the bag with fabric glue. Stitch around the flowers and leaves with freehand machine embroidery using a matching thread. To do this, lower the feed dog of the machine and set it to darning or freehand quilting. Sew accurately around the outlines of the individual motifs. If desired, you can also top stitch the lines within the rose motif. Sew on buttons and lace motifs.

5 For the outside pocket, place the two pieces of red fabric with roses right sides together and sew all around, leaving an opening at the bottom for turning. Cut away the seam allowance at the corners and turn right side out. Top stitch the upper edge with two parallel rows of stitching. Pin the pocket to the back of the bag. Sew along the bottom and side edges with two parallel rows of stitching.

6 Cut the fabric for the zip opening in half lengthways and insert the zip (see Sewing techniques, page 11). Trim to 61 x 10cm (24 x 4in). Trim the bottom and side piece to 79 x 10cm (31 x 4in). Neaten all the short sides with zigzag stitch. Cut the pink satin ribbon in half and make two bows. Join the fabric with the zip to the side piece to form a ring, sewing in ribbon bows on the right and left at the same time.

7 For the piping, iron the pink bias binding open and trim the whole length to a width of 3cm (1¼in). Prepare the piping with cotton cord (see Sewing techniques, page 10). Sew the piping to the front and back bag pieces, taking care to stitch just inside the seam allowance. Open the zip, pin the sides to the front and back, matching the markings for the mid-point from the sketch on page 48 and sew together. Trim the seam allowance to about 0.5cm (⅛in). Top stitch through the side and the front/back pieces together about 6mm (⅜in) from the edge. This will stabilise the bag and cover the seam allowance.

Finishing

Stitch the handles to the bag. Thread the rose satin ribbon through the zip pull, thread both ends together through the wooden bead and knot the ends.

Tip

If your sewing machine does not have a quilting ruler, draw the lines on the fabric with the soluble marker.

Phone Charm

Size: 11 x 7cm (4¼ x 2¾in)   Pattern 10 on page 64   Difficulty level ♡

Materials

Cotton fabric:
- ♥ 10cm (4in) turquoise and red patterned fabric
- ♥ 10cm (4in) plain fabric for backing
- ♥ Scraps of red patterned fabric

Wadding/batting:
- ♥ Double-sided iron-on wadding/batting
- ♥ Scraps of wadding/batting

Additional items:
- ♥ Scrap of pink felt
- ♥ Scraps of synthetic filling
- ♥ 25cm (10in) turquoise satin ribbon
- ♥ 2 buttons, 1cm (½in) diameter
- ♥ 2 black beads, 3mm (¼in) diameter

Cutting out

There is no seam allowance included in the pattern.

Make templates from the pattern pieces for the bird, wings and beak.

Method

1 To make the beak, fuse two pieces of felt together with the double-sided wadding/batting. Cut out the tip of the beak without seam allowance; at the end where the beak goes into the bird, add a seam allowance of 0.5cm (⅛in).

2 For the bird, draw around the template once on the wrong side of the turquoise and red patterned fabric and cut out, adding a seam allowance of 0.5cm (⅛in). Place the fabric shape on a suitably sized piece of the same material, right sides together. Insert the beak between the two layers. Stitch together all the way around with small stitches (stitch length 2), leaving an opening for turning between the markers shown on the template. Trim the second layer of fabric to the size of the front. Clip the seam allowance on the curves several times close to the stitching. Turn the bird right side out and sew up the opening by hand.

3 For the wings, draw around the template twice on the wrong side of the red patterned fabric and cut out, adding a seam allowance of 0.5 cm (⅛in). To make up the wings, place each wing piece right sides together on suitably sized pieces of the same fabric and place both layers on a piece of wadding/batting.

4 Stitch together all the way around with a small stitch length, leaving an opening for turning. Trim the wadding/batting close to the seam and cut the backing fabric to the size of the front. Cut away the seam allowance at the tips, clip the seam allowance on the curves several times close to the stitching, turn and iron. Sew up the opening and sew the wings to the body together with the buttons.

5 Sew on the two beads for the eyes. Fold the satin ribbon in half and sew the ends to the body.

Tip

For curved templates it is better to add a smaller seam allowance of 0.5cm (⅛in) than a bigger one. The smaller allowance makes it easier to sew and iron the curves.

Pencil Case

Size: 20 x 5.5cm (7¾ x 2in)   Difficulty level ♡ ♡

Materials

Cotton fabric:
- ♥ 10cm (4in) denim fabric
- ♥ 15cm (6in) pale-pink fabric

Additional items:
- ♥ 50cm (19¾in) each of 4 different turquoise and pink woven braids, 12mm (½in) wide
- ♥ 15cm (6in) rose-pink satin ribbon
- ♥ 2m (79in) double-sided iron-on adhesive tape for fabrics
- ♥ 1 zip, 25cm (9¾in) long
- ♥ 1 pompom
- ♥ Water-soluble marker

Cutting out

A seam allowance of 0.75cm (¼in) or 1cm (½in) is included in the measurements.

From the denim, cut out:
- ♥ 2 pieces 22 x 7.5cm (8¾ x 3in)

From the pale-pink fabric, cut out:
- ♥ 1 piece 21.5 x 12cm (8½ x 4¾in)

Method

1 Neaten all the edges of the denim pieces with zigzag stitch. On each one, draw a line with the magic marker 1cm (½in) away from one long edge and parallel to it. Fold the seam allowance for the zip to the wrong side along this line and tack in place.

2 Tack the zip under the fabric and stitch in place using the zipper foot. Remove the tacking threads (see Sewing techniques, page 11).

3 Cut two 22cm (8¾in) lengths of each of the braids. Stick the double-sided adhesive tape to the back of the first braid and press it firmly in place with a fingernail. Remove the backing paper from the other side of the tape and fasten the braid to the denim. Begin with the first strip close to the seam of the zip.

4 Top stitch along the edges of the braids. Place the two pieces of the pencil case right sides together and sew together along the bottom edge. Leave the zip open about 15cm (6in) for turning.

5 For version 1 (on the right of the photogtaph), pin the seams together at each end. Fold 10cm (4in) satin ribbon in half and insert it between the layers of fabric. Stitch the side seams.

6 To make the lining, fold the rose-pink fabric in half, right sides together and sew up the side seams. Fold 1cm (½in) of fabric to the wrong side along the top edges. Insert the lining into the pencil case and sew it to the zip by hand.

7 For version 2 (on the left of the photograph), fold the case so the seam runs along on top of the zip and pin in place. Fold 10cm (4in) of satin ribbon in half and insert it between the layers of fabric. Stitch the side seams. For the lining, fold 1cm (½in) of fabric to the wrong side of the long edges. Fold both long edges over almost to the middle and stitch the side seams. Insert the lining into the pencil case and sew it to the zip by hand.

8 As an embellishment, thread the remainder of the satin ribbon through the zip pull and knot the ends. Glue a pompom to the end.

Materials

Cotton fabric:
- ♥ 20cm (7¾in) pink fabric
- ♥ 20cm (7¾in) white patterned fabric
- ♥ 20cm (7¾in) pink and white spotted fabric

Wadding/batting:
- ♥ 20cm (7¾in) iron-on wadding/batting

Additional items:
- ♥ 50cm (19¾in) pink frill edging
- ♥ 25cm (9¾in) small pompom braid
- ♥ 25cm (9¾in) pink and white checked bias binding
- ♥ 10cm (4in) white satin ribbon
- ♥ 1 zip, 25cm (9¾in) long
- ♥ 1 button, 1.5cm (¾in) diameter
- ♥ 1 pink crocheted flower
- ♥ Water-soluble marker

Cutting out

A seam allowance of 0.75cm (¼in) or 1cm (½in) (for the zip) is included in the measurements.

From the pink fabric, cut out:
- ♥ 2 pieces 23 x 19cm (9 x 7½in) for the bag

From the white patterned fabric, cut out:
- ♥ 1 piece 23 x 16cm (9 x 6¼in) for the flap

From the pink and white spotted fabric, cut out:
- ♥ 2 pieces 22.5 x 18.5cm (9 x 7¼in) for the lining

From the wadding/batting, cut out:
- ♥ 2 pieces 23 x 18cm (9 x 7in) for the bag
- ♥ 1 piece 23 x 16cm (9 x 6¼in) for the flap

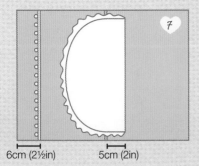

6cm (2½in)   5cm (2in)

Make-up Bag

Size: 21 x 14cm (8¼ x 5½in)   **Pattern 11 on page 64**   **Difficulty level** ♡ ♡

Method

1 Fuse the iron-on wadding/batting to the wrong side of the fabric pieces for the bag and flap. There should be 1cm (½in) left without wadding/batting at the top edges of the bag where the zip will go.

2 On the right side of the pink and white spotted fabric, draw a line with the magic marker 1cm (½in) from the edge for the zip. Fold the seam allowance to the wrong side along this line and tack in place. Tack the zip under the fabric and stitch in place using the zipper foot. Remove the tacking threads (see Sewing techniques, page 11).

3 For the flap, transfer the pattern to the white patterned fabric and cut out the rough shape. Pin right sides together on the prepared flap piece. Stitch together along the curved edge. Trim both layers close to the stitching. Clip the seam allowance on the curve several times close to the stitching and turn the flap right side out.

4 Pin the frill edging around the curve underneath the flap and stitch close to the edge.

5 Pin the flap to one part of the bag with the flap's straight edge, 5cm (2in) above the top edge of the bag. Sew the pompom braid to the other part of the bag, 6cm (2½in) from the lower edge (see sketch, bottom left).

6 Top stitch the bias binding over the seam that attaches the flap to the bag.

7 Place the two parts of the bag right sides together, leaving the zip open for turning. Sew together all the way around. To finish the base, sew across the bottom corners 3cm (1¼in) from the corner, referring to the sketch on page 34.

8 To make the lining, place the two pieces of pink fabric right sides together and sew up the side and bottom seams. Sew across the corners, as you did for the bag. Fold 1cm (½in) of fabric along the top edge to the wrong side. Insert the lining into the bag and sew it to the zip by hand.

9 Tie the satin ribbon into a loop and sew it in place under the middle of the flap. Sew the button to the crocheted flower then sew both to the bag by hand.

Templates

1
Tea Cup Mug Rug

2
Egg Cosies

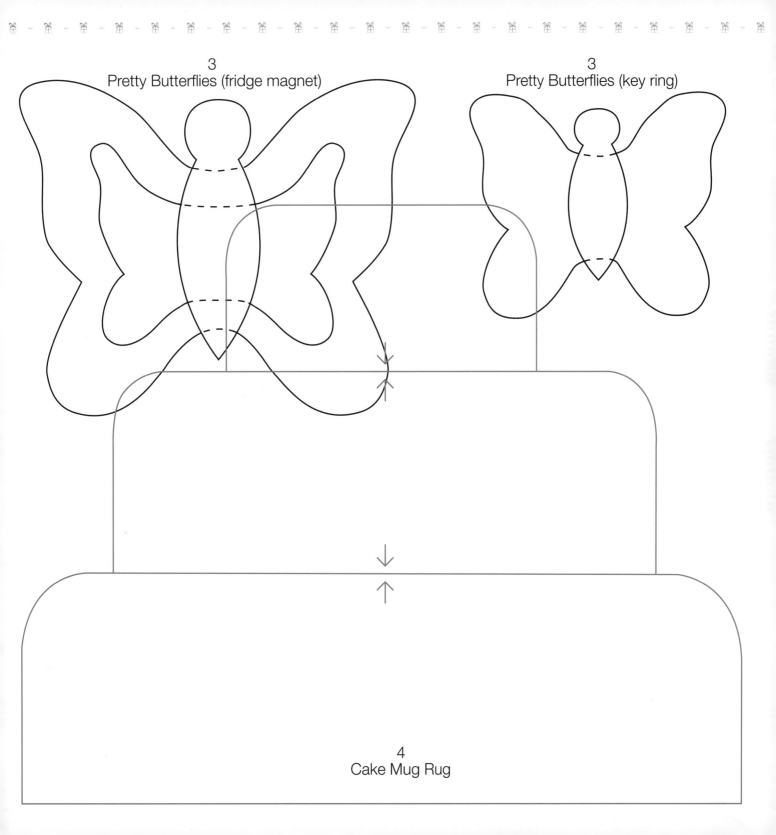

3
Pretty Butterflies (fridge magnet)

3
Pretty Butterflies (key ring)

4
Cake Mug Rug

6
Lovely Pillow

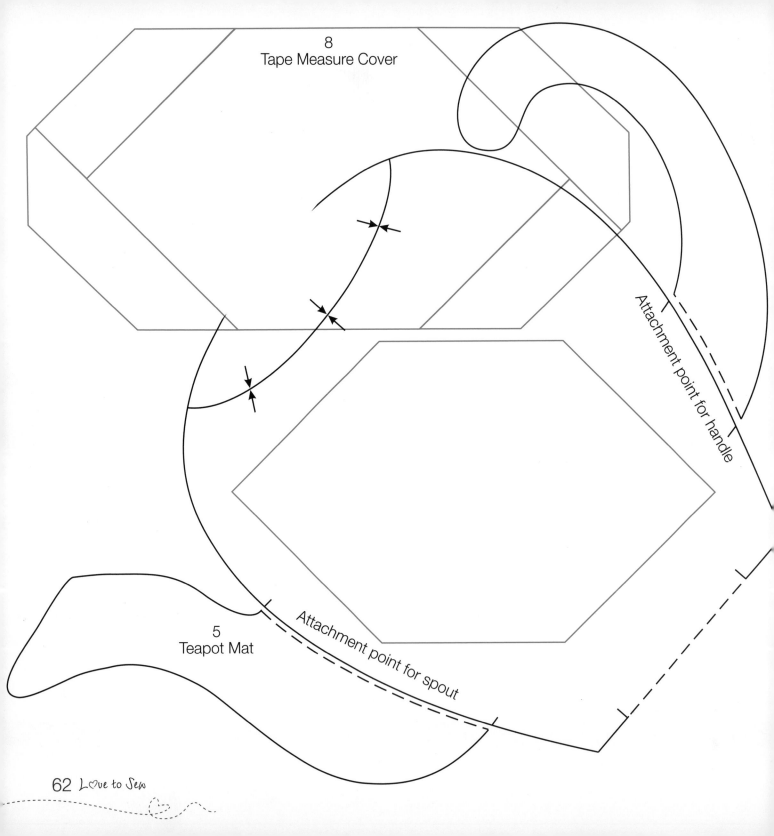

8
Tape Measure Cover

Attachment point for handle

5
Teapot Mat

Attachment point for spout

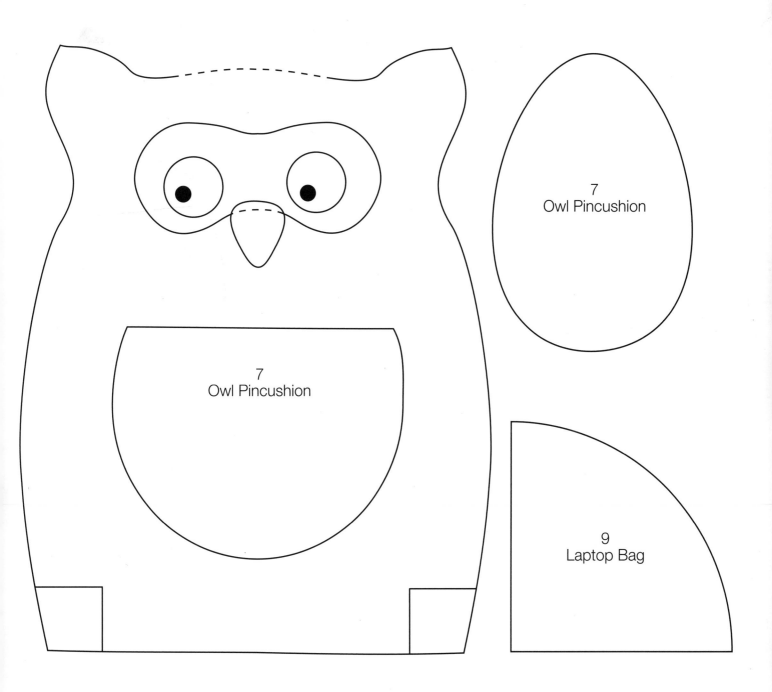

7
Owl Pincushion

7
Owl Pincushion

9
Laptop Bag

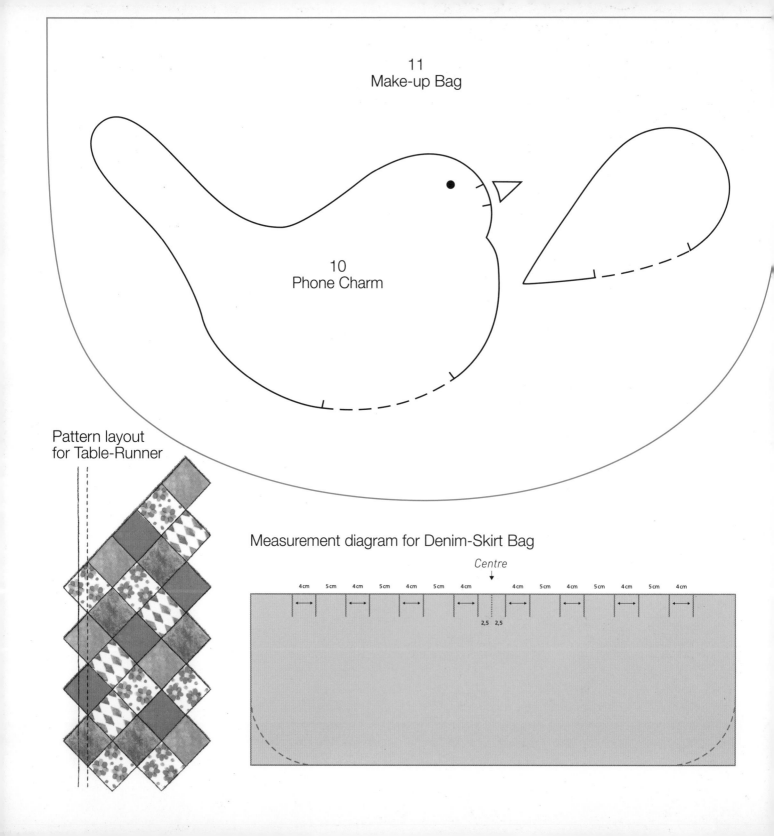

11
Make-up Bag

10
Phone Charm

Pattern layout
for Table-Runner

Measurement diagram for Denim-Skirt Bag

Centre

4cm 5cm 4cm 5cm 4cm 5cm 4cm   4cm 5cm 4cm 5cm 4cm 5cm 4cm

2,5 2,5